# URSA

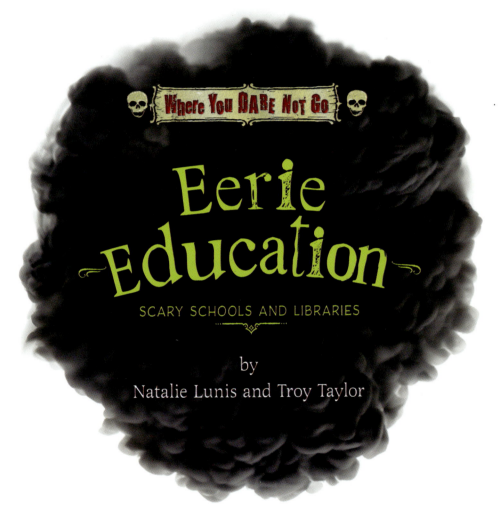

### Where You DARE Not Go

# Eerie Education

SCARY SCHOOLS AND LIBRARIES

by
Natalie Lunis and Troy Taylor

BEARPORT
PUBLISHING

Minneapolis, Minnesota

**Credits**

Cover and title page, © LittleEvilYor/Shutterstock, © The American Explorer/Shutterstock, © Goga_s/Shutterstock, © Fer Gregory/Shutterstock, © Inmaculada Blanca/Shutterstock, and © Studio Romantic/Shutterstock; 4, © Harry Kasyanov/Adobe Stock, © Viorika/iStock, and © Bastetamn/iStock; 6, © nancykennedy/iStock and © S6336s/Creative Commons Attribution-Share Alike 4.0 International; 8, © Nyttend/Wikimedia Commons; 9, © Donna Beeler/Shutterstock and © https://www.willardghost.com/; 10, © Larry D. Moore/Creative Commons Attribution 4.0 International, © Public Domain/Wikimedia Commons, and © Herbert Rose Barraud/Wikimedia Commons; 12, © Emil Boehl/Wikimedia Commons; 13, © Public Domain/Wikimedia Commons and © LanKS/Shutterstock; 14, © Nobel Foundation/Wikimedia Commons and © Loodog/Creative Commons Attribution-Share Alike 3.0 Unported; 15, © Alice Boughton/United States Library of Congress's Prints and Photographs division; 16, © Nyttend/Wikimedia Commons; 17, © Everett Collection/Shutterstock, © Africa Studio/Shutterstock, and © schankz/Shutterstock; 18, © csfotoimages/iStock; 19, © studiovin/Shutterstock and © Donna Beeler/Shutterstock; 20, © PhotoFlow/Alamy; 21, © 2RHAWDP/Alamy and © Brand Library/Wikimedia Commons; 23, © Jordan M. McAlister/Flickr; 24, © Schlitzer90/Creative Commons Attribution-Share Alike 3.0 Unported; 26, © Victor Koval/Shutterstock and © 2017 Google/Map data 2017 Google; 27, © RAY-BON/Shutterstock; 28, © John Margolies/United States Library of Congress's Prints and Photographs division; 29, © 2021 Google/Map data 2021 Google; 30, © Armen/Creative Commons Attribution-Share Alike 4.0 International and © OneDayOneImage/Alamy; 32, © Riofriotex/Creative Commons Attribution-Share Alike 4.0 International; 33, © photovova/Shutterstock, © Plateresca/Shutterstock, and © CapturePB/Shutterstock; 34, © Brian Gray / Contributor/Getty Images; 35, © Public Domain/Wikimedia Commons; 36, © Tichnor Brothers/Wikimedia Commons; 37, © Tawatchai chaimongkon/Shutterstock and © Silvio Russo/Shutterstock; 38, © Suzette Leg Anthony/Shutterstock and © David Shamma/Creative Commons Attribution-Share Alike 2.0 Generic; 39, © Jaroslaw Grudzinski/Shutterstock and © Beautiful landscape/Shutterstock; 40, © Bruce H. Cox/Los Angeles Times Photographic Collection; 41, © leolintang/Shutterstock and © Loke Yek Mang/Shutterstock.

**Bearport Publishing Company Product Development Team**

President: Jen Jenson; Director of Product Development: Spencer Brinker; Managing Editor: Allison Juda; Associate Editor: Naomi Reich; Associate Editor: Tiana Tran; Art Director: Colin O'Dea; Designer: Kim Jones; Designer: Kayla Eggert; Product Development Assistant: Owen Hamlin

**Statement on Usage of Generative Artificial Intelligence**

Bearport Publishing remains committed to publishing high-quality nonfiction books. Therefore, we restrict the use of generative AI to ensure accuracy of all text and visual components pertaining to a book's subject. See BearportPublishing.com for details.

*Library of Congress Cataloging-in-Publication Data*

Names: Lunis, Natalie, author. | Taylor, Troy, 1966- author.
Title: Eerie education : scary schools and libraries / by Natalie Lunis and Troy Taylor.
Description: Minneapolis, Minnesota : Bearport Publishing, [2025] | Series: Where you dare not go | Includes bibliographical references and index.
Identifiers: LCCN 2024004277 (print) | LCCN 2024004278 (ebook) | ISBN 9798892320726 (library binding) | ISBN 9798892326049 (paperback) | ISBN 9798892322058 (ebook)
Subjects: LCSH: Haunted schools--United States--Juvenile literature.
Classification: LCC BF1478 .L85 2025 (print) | LCC BF1478 (ebook) | DDC 133.1/22--dc23/eng/20240315
LC record available at https://lccn.loc.gov/2024004277
LC ebook record available at https://lccn.loc.gov/2024004278

Copyright © 2025 Bearport Publishing Company. All rights reserved. No part of this publication may be reproduced in whole or in part, stored in any retrieval system, or transmitted in any form or by any means, electronic, mechanical, photocopying, recording, or otherwise, without written permission from the publisher. Bearport Publishing is a division of Chrysalis Education Group.

For more information, write to Bearport Publishing, 5357 Penn Avenue South, Minneapolis, MN 55419.

# Contents

A Scary Education .................... 4
The Ghost in the Garden .................... 6
The Grey Lady .................... 8
The Haunted Library .................... 10
Still at School .................... 12
A Playwright's Comeback .................... 14
A Collection of Ghosts .................... 16
The Brown Suit Man .................... 18
An Eerie Voice .................... 20
An Unhappy Ending .................... 22
The Girl in the Window .................... 24
Touched by Death .................... 26
Spirits on the Move .................... 28
Haunted in Fact and Fiction .................... 30
Music from Beyond .................... 32
A Deadly Promise .................... 34
A Playful Ghost .................... 36
Trouble in the Bell Tower .................... 38
Afraid of the Water .................... 40

A World of . . . Eerie Education .................... 42
Glossary .................... 44
Read More .................... 46
Learn More Online .................... 46
Index .................... 47

# A Scary Education

Schools and libraries are a normal part of every student's life. But what happens when you hear strange noises coming from empty, locked classrooms? Was that a tall shadow moving between the dusty shelves in the library's dark corner? You've heard rumors of ghosts at your school. Could some former students still be stuck there . . . forever?

# The Ghost in the Garden

## BARD COLLEGE
### ANNANDALE-ON-HUDSON, NEW YORK

Students at Bard College are lucky to go to a school with a gardenlike campus overlooking the Hudson River. The spot is so beautiful that one girl, it seems, decided to return to it after death—and hasn't left since. . . .

Blithewood Mansion

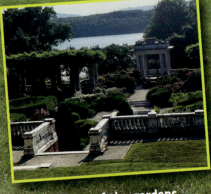

A view of the gardens

In 1899, Captain Andrew C. Zabriskie bought a large piece of property overlooking the Hudson River. There, he built a grand white mansion to use as a summer home for his family. He put in beautiful gardens and walkways, many with breathtaking views of the river. Because the property had been formerly known as Blithewood, everyone called the new house Blithewood Mansion.

Just over 50 years later, in 1951, the captain's son gave Blithewood Mansion to nearby Bard College. Since then, students and teachers have seen a strange girl wandering both outside and inside the house, which is now used by professors who teach economics.

The girl, who seems to be somewhere between 8 and 12 years old, is believed to be Captain Zabriskie's daughter. People say that one winter night she fell to her death from a window of her family's New York City apartment. Because she disliked the big city, she is now reported to spend all her time as a ghost at her family's beautiful home on the river.

Captain Zabriskie had four statues of his daughter made for the gardens, but only three remain. There is an empty spot where the fourth statue once stood. Some say that the young girl haunts the garden in the form of this statue.

# The Grey Lady

## WILLARD LIBRARY, EVANSVILLE, INDIANA

Willard Carpenter was a wealthy man who lived in Evansville in the 1800s. When he died in 1883, he left much of his fortune to the town so that a huge library could be built. This angered his daughter, Louise, who wanted the fortune for herself. In 1908, Louise died—and reportedly came back from the dead to haunt the Willard Library. Today, her ghost is known as the Grey Lady.

The Willard Library

A custodian first saw Louise's ghost in the library in 1937. While working in the basement, he spotted the figure of a woman in a long grey dress, grey shawl, and grey veil. The custodian was so scared he dropped the flashlight he was holding. The flashlight flickered off, and when he turned it back on, the woman had vanished!

Since then, many other staff members have spotted the Grey Lady. One librarian said that while construction work was being done in the building, the ghost followed her home! After the construction was finished, the Grey Lady came back to the library—and has been there ever since.

Because so many people around the country are interested in the Grey Lady, the library has installed ghost cams. Now, everyone can watch for the ghost on the internet.

A view of the library stairs from the ghost cam

# The Haunted Library

## BAYLOR UNIVERSITY, WACO, TEXAS

Elizabeth Barrett Browning is a famous English poet. She never set foot in the United States, yet her ghost is said to haunt the library of a university in Texas.

Browning Library at Baylor University

Elizabeth Barrett Browning

Robert Browning

As a young woman, Elizabeth Barrett was often ill. She spent her days writing letters and poetry in her bedroom at her family's home in London. Her life changed in 1845 when another young poet named Robert Browning visited her there.

During their first meeting, Robert told Elizabeth how much he loved her poems. A year later, he and Elizabeth married and moved to Italy. There, the two lived happily, often working side by side, until Elizabeth's death in 1861.

Almost a hundred years later, a professor of English at Baylor University in Waco, Texas, helped the school gather a large collection of the Brownings' letters and manuscripts. The school also collected furniture, paintings, and jewelry that had belonged to the poets and built a beautiful library to hold the items. Today, people who spend time in the building say Elizabeth's ghost can be found there as well. Some think she cannot stay away from the belongings and writings that meant so much to her. Others recall that in one of her most famous poems, Elizabeth declares she will love her husband even more after death. Does she keep her promise by forever searching for him?

Among the objects in the library are locks of Robert's and Elizabeth's hair.

# Still at School

### REID MEMORIAL LIBRARY, GODFREY, ILLINOIS

Some people are so passionate about what they do that they show up to their workplaces even if they are sick. However, a schoolteacher and principal named Harriet Haskell showed up to work even after she had died! Today, her ghost remains at the school where she spent much of her life.

Monticello Seminary

In 1867, Harriet became the principal of a women's college in Illinois called the Monticello Seminary. She was beloved by her students. When Harriet died in 1907, former students from all around the country came back to Illinois for her funeral.

Harriet Haskell

Many years later, in 1971, the Monticello Seminary became Lewis and Clark Community College. The previous school's chapel—Harriet's favorite room— was turned into a library. It is said that Harriet's spirit lives on in this room. Security guards claim they hear the elevator run at night when nobody else is in the building. Sometimes, lights turn on and off and water faucets run for no reason. Some librarians have even seen Harriet's ghost! The ghost is dressed in clothes much like the ones Harriet would have worn in the 1800s.

Why did Harriet's spirit start appearing in the library? No one knows for sure. Although the events are spooky, everyone is happy that Harriet is still around. They feel as though she's watching over the school she loved.

Lilacs

Some people say they can smell lilacs in the library when no one else is around. This is the scent of a perfume Harriet wore when she was alive.

# A Playwright's Comeback

## BOSTON UNIVERSITY
## BOSTON, MASSACHUSETTS

While in college, many students study the work of famous writers from the past. Some students at a large school in the heart of Boston get to do even more—they live with one.

Shelton Hall

Playwright Eugene O'Neill

In some ways, Shelton Hall is like any other college dormitory. The students there spend their time studying, hanging out with friends, listening to music, and doing laundry or other day-to-day tasks.

In other ways, however, Shelton Hall is different from other student housing. Up on the fourth floor, the elevator often stops for no reason at all. There are knocks on the doors when no one is out in the hallway. Sometimes at night, a strong wind blows down the hall.

Surprisingly, the students who live in Shelton Hall have an explanation for the strange events. Before the building became a dormitory, it was the Shelton Hotel. For two years, Eugene O'Neill, one of America's greatest playwrights, lived in a room on the fourth floor. He died there in 1953. Since then, people claim he has been haunting the hallway. His presence has not scared young people away, however. In fact, it has done the opposite. The fourth floor—now known as the Writers' Corridor—attracts writing students who hope to become better at their craft by meeting up with O'Neill's spirit.

Students put up a bulletin board in the fourth-floor hallway so that they can post notes about the strange things they have seen. So far, O'Neill's ghost has not added any messages of his own.

# A Collection of Ghosts

## CARNEGIE LIBRARY
## PARKERSBURG, WEST VIRGINIA

An abandoned library in West Virginia spent years collecting dust before a bookstore moved into the space. Then, the building began providing a wonderful home for books—and many ghosts.

The Carnegie Library became the Trans-Allegheny Bookstore.

In 1904, wealthy businessman Andrew Carnegie donated thousands of dollars to the town of Parkersburg in West Virginia to build a library. The library closed in 1976 and sat empty until 1985, when it was turned into the Trans-Allegheny Bookstore.

The building became one of the largest used bookstores in West Virginia—and possibly the most haunted. Several different ghosts were said to be living there, including three women, a well-dressed man, a little girl, and three cats. Some people have claimed that they tripped over a cat on the circular iron staircase, only to turn back and find nothing there.

Visitors saw other signs of hauntings. Books flew off the shelves, overhead lamps swayed back and forth, and lights flickered on and off. The former library was a great place to buy books, but some customers left quickly after finding ghosts instead!

One of the bookstore's ghosts was believed to be a newspaper reporter who was murdered in her home in 1989. She had spent much of her time digging for facts at the old Carnegie Library. Perhaps after her death, she decided to return to the building she knew so well.

# The Brown Suit Man

## THE UNIVERSITY OF TAMPA, TAMPA, FLORIDA

Students who attend the University of Tampa lead busy lives. A little more than a hundred years ago, however, people came to the same spot to relax and have fun. At least one of them might still be coming back—unaware of the changes that have taken place since his time.

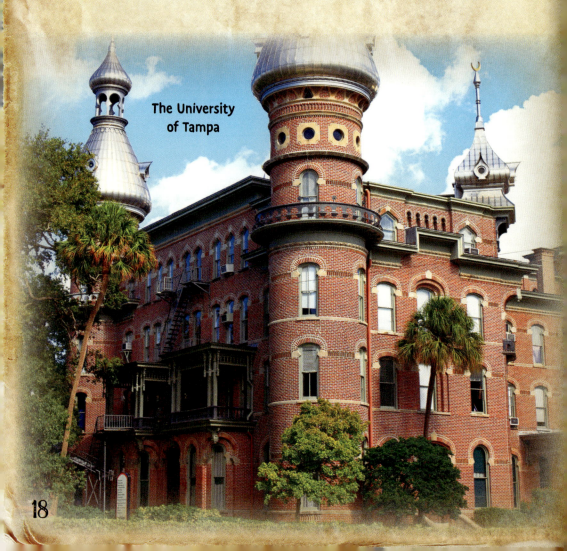

The University of Tampa

Even though they might not have seen him, most students at the University of Tampa know all about a strange person who could not possibly belong at the school. Why? According to those who have spotted him, the man is unforgettable. He wears an old-fashioned, brown three-piece suit and has glowing red eyes. He also appears and disappears suddenly on a stairway.

Because of his clothing, the figure has become known as the Brown Suit Man. The strange man's clothing also offers a clue to whom he might be and why he might sometimes show up on campus. Before the property in downtown Tampa became the site of the school, it was the Tampa Bay Hotel. Photos from the late 1800s show the hotel's beautiful and spacious lobby. They also show a group of men talking and relaxing on a high-ceilinged porch. Could the Brown Suit Man be one of them—a ghost who returns in an attempt to relive the good times of the past?

Ghostly sounds remind some students of the school's past as a hotel. In one area where a casino once stood, some have heard the sound of rolling dice.

# An Eerie Voice

## BRAND LIBRARY, GLENDALE, CALIFORNIA

In 1904, Leslie Coombs Brand built a beautiful white mansion. Brand died in 1925 and donated his home to the town of Glendale, California, so it could be used as a library. Some people believe he returned to the library after his death.

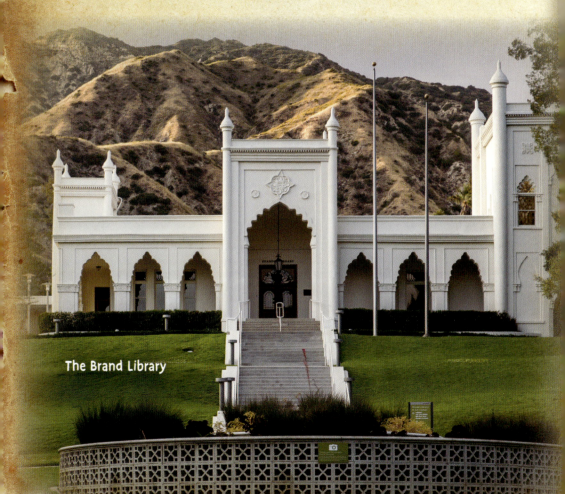

The Brand Library

Many staff members say Brand's spirit sometimes speaks in a low voice or makes sudden, unsettling appearances. One day, librarian Joseph Fuchs saw a man walk up a set of stairs not open to the public. Before Joseph had a chance to say something, the man disappeared. The librarian couldn't believe his eyes. Another time, he was working alone in the library at night when he heard a low, moaning voice say "Joe." Scared out of his wits, Joseph quickly ran out of the building.

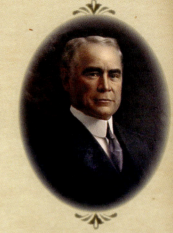
Leslie Coombs Brand

The strange sounds and eerie visions have affected other library workers, too. The library's custodians refuse to work alone at night. They're afraid they might see the ghost of Leslie Coombs Brand—the man who refuses to leave his former home.

The Brand family mausoleum

Not far from the Brand Library is a small cemetery. Leslie Coombs Brand is buried there in a mausoleum shaped like a pyramid.

# An Unhappy Ending

## AUGUSTA STATE UNIVERSITY
## AUGUSTA, GEORGIA

At a school in Georgia, two ghostly voices are heard sharply disagreeing. What are these troubled spirits arguing about? Why have they been unable to find peace so many years after their deaths?

Bellevue Hall at Augusta State University

In 1861, America's northern and southern states were fighting the Civil War. Twenty-one-year-old Emily Galt was engaged to a young man, but the two could not stay together. The young man had decided to go off and join the Confederate Army. No matter how much Emily argued and pleaded with him, he refused to change his mind. He went to war, and Emily's worst fears came true. He was killed in battle.

Emily's home—the place where she and the young man argued—later became part of Augusta State University. Those who work and study in the building, known today as Bellevue Hall, have heard two people arguing, but the couple can never be found. Students and faculty have also seen Emily's name etched on the glass of a second-floor window. According to the stories that are told on campus, Emily used her diamond engagement ring to scratch the letters into the windowpane. Shortly after she learned of her fiancé's death, she threw herself from the window. Ever since, she and the young man seem unable to stop repeating the upsetting final moments they spent together.

**Did Emily scratch her name into a window?**

Other strange activity also suggests that Emily's former home is haunted. Phones sometimes ring for no reason, and doors open and close. A television is also said to turn itself on and off.

# The Girl in the Window

## MILLICENT LIBRARY
### FAIRHAVEN, MASSACHUSETTS

The colorful stained-glass window in a library in Massachusetts shows a beautiful young woman whose life was cut short. Could she be haunting the place that was built as a memorial to her?

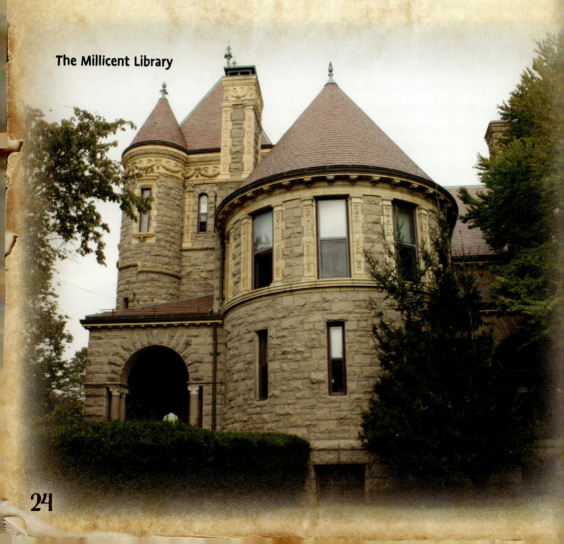

The Millicent Library

In 1890, Henry Huttleston Rogers built a magnificent library and named it after his daughter, Millicent, who had died when she was just 17 years old. The library has a huge stained-glass window that includes a portrait of Millicent. The girl remains in the library in another way, too—as a ghost. Patrons claim to have heard Millicent laughing and seen her dancing in the aisles between the bookshelves.

And Millicent may not be the only ghost in the library. Some people say they have also seen a woman dressed in black running her fingers along the bookshelves. As soon as she is spotted, she vanishes.

One room in the library holds several paintings of members of the Rogers family. Cold spots are often reported near the pictures. Some say that if a person speaks directly to the portraits of Millicent's dead family members, the faces in the pictures will react to what is being said!

Since Millicent loved reading poetry, the library's stained-glass window shows her as the Muse of Poetry. According to Greek legends, muses inspired writers and artists in their work. It is said that the girl in the window inspired many great writers, including Mark Twain, whose books can be found on the library's shelves.

# Touched by Death

## FORDHAM UNIVERSITY, BRONX, NEW YORK

College students are usually young and healthy. So why do those who live in a beautiful old dormitory sometimes feel as if they are surrounded by death?

Fordham University

Finlay Hall

With its tall trees and castlelike buildings that cast long shadows in the late afternoon, Fordham University looks like a place that might be haunted. In fact, many people say several spots on campus are often visited by ghosts. Perhaps the scariest of these is a dormitory called Finlay Hall.

In the early 1900s, Finlay Hall did not serve as a home for students as it does today. Instead, the building held a medical school—with a morgue full of dead bodies in the basement. Those who live in Finlay now believe that this fact explains why they sometimes wake up with the feeling that an icy hand is grabbing their throat.

The building's past may also explain other creepy happenings. In some especially large rooms with lofts, students sometimes wake up to see ghostly faces staring down at them. As everyone in Finlay Hall knows, the balcony-like structures were the places where medical students once stood as they observed professors and more advanced students cut into corpses in order to learn about the human body.

According to one story, a security guard observed a high level of ghostly activity one night as he took a break in the basement of Finlay Hall. Doors slammed shut and chairs crashed against the walls on their own. The guard was so scared that he quit that night and never returned.

# Spirits on the Move

## PARMLY BILLINGS LIBRARY
### BILLINGS, MONTANA

The Parmly Billings Library was named in honor of the son of Frederick Billings, the town's founder. Billings's son, Parmly, died suddenly when he was only 25 years old. Over the years, the library moved to different buildings. All the while, various ghosts have been reported in the different locations. Apparently, the spirits moved along with the books!

The original Billings Library

The original Parmly Billings Library was built in 1901. By 1969, the growing community needed a larger library, so town leaders chose a large red brick building as the new location. It is said that the original castle-like building was haunted. It is also said that when the books and furniture from the old library were moved to the new one, the ghosts moved, too.

Staff members and visitors saw a number of spirits in the red brick library, including a girl in a frilly dress and a man wearing a jean jacket. One library employee saw a very tall spirit that looked like a column of smoke. Just after it was seen, the spirit disappeared into thin air.

Who are these ghosts? Could they be staff members or former library patrons who died long ago? No one knows, but the spirits seem content to be in the Billings Library—no matter where it's located.

In 2014, the Billings Library moved again. The staff brought along all the old books and furniture from the previous library. Soon after, ghosts were being reported in the new building!

The newest Billings Library

# Haunted in Fact and Fiction

## BENNINGTON COLLEGE
### BENNINGTON, VERMONT

In the late 1950s, author Shirley Jackson wrote a novel called *The Haunting of Hill House*. The book became one of the most famous horror stories ever written. Although it is fiction, Jackson's work was based on a very real house that belonged to the college that was just down the street from her home.

Jennings Hall at Bennington College

Author Shirley Jackson

Jennings Hall is a 40-room house that became Bennington College's music building in 1939. Music classes are held there, and students use small practice rooms to play the piano or violin or to work on their singing. The sounds of music are not the only ones heard in this beautiful New England mansion, however. People have also reported hearing footsteps and whispers inside—even though no one was around.

In 1945, Shirley Jackson came to Bennington because her husband had been hired to teach there. The young couple's house was quite close to Jennings Hall. It is believed that the stories about the building and the strange happenings inside gave Jackson the idea for her own haunted house book.

It is also almost certain that Jackson, like other people at Bennington, thought the building became even spookier in 1946. During that year, a music student named Paula Welden disappeared. She was last seen heading out of town. Did she run away, or was she murdered—only to return to Jennings Hall as a ghost? To this day, no one knows what really happened to her.

The Haunting of Hill House is about four people who agree to spend time at a house that is thought to be haunted. They are there to discover whether the stories people tell about it are true or not.

# Music from Beyond

## JULIA IDESON LIBRARY, HOUSTON, TEXAS

Located in downtown Houston is the Julia Ideson Library, an old three-story building with many mysteries. One of the mysteries involves two resident ghosts—a former library worker who died in the building in 1936 and his loyal dog. Are the ghosts refusing to leave the library they lived in decades ago?

The Julia Ideson Library

**L**ong ago, the Julia Ideson Library was home to Jacob Frank Cramer, an elderly man who worked as a night watchman, gardener, and handyman for the library. Jacob and his German shepherd, Petey, lived in the library's basement. At night, when the library was closed, he and the dog would climb the stairs to the top floor. Then, Jacob would play his violin, filling the building with music.

Today, years after their deaths, Jacob and Petey may still live in the library. Visitors and staff claim to have heard the *click-click-click* of a dog's nails tapping on the tile floors. When they look for the source of the sound, there is no dog to be found. Others say that sheet music, normally kept in a locked room, is sometimes found scattered around the library.

Creepiest of all, however, is when people hear faint violin music playing throughout the library. Could it be Jacob, still wanting to fill the building with the beautiful music he made when he was alive?

The sound of eerie violin music is usually heard in the library on days when the weather is gloomy.

# A Deadly Promise

## KENYON COLLEGE, GAMBIER, OHIO

More than a hundred years ago, a college student in Ohio died while proving his trust in his schoolmates. Today, students turn out every year to show that although he is gone, he is not forgotten.

Kenyon College

On October 28, 1905, Stuart Pierson was at college, preparing himself for a test. He was not about to take an exam in math, science, or history, however. Instead, he wanted to show that he was willing to place complete trust in the members of a fraternity called Delta Kappa Epsilon, or DKE for short. If he passed the test, the fraternity brothers would allow him to join their club and live in their house on campus.

**Stuart Pierson**

Stuart did as he was told. He followed a group of students to a train trestle and lay down on the tracks. The students instructed him to stay there until they returned. When they came back, they had a terrible shock. A train had unexpectedly come through and killed Stuart.

Since then, Stuart is remembered every year on the anniversary of his death. Members of DKE carry a coffin filled with stones to the spot where he died. Stuart is also said to appear on that day. People claim they have seen him looking out of a window on the fourth floor of the fraternity house—finally at home in the building where he had wanted to live.

Stuart also haunts the DKE house at other times of the year. Windows open and close, and his footsteps are sometimes heard on the top floor.

# A Playful Ghost

## BRIDGEPORT PUBLIC LIBRARY
## BRIDGEPORT, CONNECTICUT

About 40 years after the Bridgeport Public Library opened in 1881, a new library was built where the old one stood—and a ghost moved right into the new building. Staff members describe her as a helpful spirit who puts books back on the shelves. However, she is also known as a prankster.

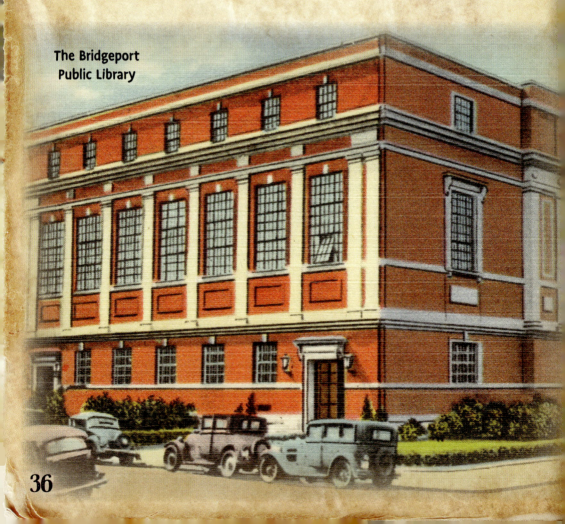

The Bridgeport Public Library

Late one night in February 2006, the library director was called at his home because the library's alarm had gone off. Thinking someone might have broken into the building, he rushed there. When he got to the library, he saw that all the lights on the fifth floor were on and a door that had been closed was open. He turned off the lights, closed the door, and went back home.

About an hour after he left, the alarm went off again. This time, several police officers came to search the library. When they looked around the building, they saw that the lights had been turned on again and the door was open. The officers also thought they heard the sound of someone flipping the pages of a book— but there was nobody else in the building. Was it the library's ghost causing some late-night mischief?

Although library workers don't know what their ghostly helper was called when she was alive, they have named her Lola.

# Trouble in the Bell Tower

## SAN FRANCISCO ART INSTITUTE
## SAN FRANCISCO, CALIFORNIA

What would you expect to hear in an old bell tower? Most people would say the deep, rich clanging of a bell. Yet that's not what those who have been inside the bell tower of a famous art school would say. According to them, what stands out is the sound of unhappy ghosts!

The San Francisco Art Institute

The bell tower

In 1947, Bill Morehouse was a student at the Art Institute of San Francisco. To help make ends meet, he took a job as a night watchman and decided to sleep in the Institute's bell tower. Starting on his first night, strange noises made him wonder if someone—or something—else was there as well. As he lay in bed, he heard footsteps coming up the tower's staircase. Then, he heard a door open. More sounds made him think someone was passing through his room, turning around, and closing the door.

For a long time, Bill continued to hear the footsteps. Later, other strange events occurred, adding to people's belief that the school was haunted. In a sculpture studio one night, all the power tools turned on by themselves. Finally, a team of psychics was called in. One of them saw an image of a graveyard—suggesting that disturbed spirits were the source of the troubles. Research later proved that the school had, in fact, been built on the grounds of an old cemetery.

Some of the psychics who investigated the school had a different idea. They thought that the haunting was caused by the spirits of art students who were not able to produce the great artwork that they had hoped to create.

# Afraid of the Water

## RAMONA CONVENT SECONDARY SCHOOL
### ALHAMBRA, CALIFORNIA

Often, there is more than one ghost at work in a place that is truly haunted. That is the case at one high school in California. At least 3 ghosts are said to roam through different parts of the 110-year-old campus.

Ramona Convent Secondary School

Ramona Convent Secondary School is one of the oldest high schools in California. So it is not surprising that this all-girls school is home to more than one ghost—or at least more than one ghost story.

According to reports, the ghostly figure of a nun has been seen throughout the school. White and glowing, the spirit floats from room to room and is most often seen in the library. Another spirit is not seen at all. Instead, it is heard in the form of piano playing. The music fills the air, even though there is no one around who could be causing it.

The most frightening ghost of all haunts the school's swimming pool. People say a girl accidentally drowned there. They also say that since that tragic event, swimmers have sometimes felt someone pulling on their leg from underneath the water, as if trying to ask for help. Reportedly, some students are so frightened when they hear the story that they refuse to go into the pool.

In 1987, an earthquake damaged several buildings at the school. People say that is roughly the same time when the stories of the ghostly piano playing and the haunted pool began. Is it possible that the shaking of the earth disturbed the ghosts?

# A World of...

# Eerie Education

# Glossary

**anniversary** a date that marks something that happened on the same day in the past

**campus** the land and building or buildings that make up a school

**casino** a place where people gamble by playing cards and other kinds of games

**chapel** a building or room used for praying

**Civil War** the war in the United States between the southern states and the northern states, which lasted from 1861 to 1865

**coffin** a container in which a dead person is placed for burial

**cold spots** small areas where the air feels colder than the air around them, thought by some to be caused by the presence of ghosts

**Confederate Army** the army that fought for the southern states during the Civil War

**convent** a place where nuns live and work

**corpses** dead bodies

**corridor** a hallway

**custodian** a person who cleans and takes care of a building

**donated** gave as a gift

**dormitory** a building with rooms where students live and sleep on a college campus

**economics** the study of how goods are bought and sold

**engagement ring** a ring given by one person to another to show that the couple is going to get married

**faculty** teachers in a school or college

**fiancé** the man whom a woman is going to marry

**founder** a person who establishes a town or city

**fraternity** a group of students who form a club and often live together at a college

**ghost cams** cameras set up to record paranormal activity, such as the movements of a ghost

**legends** stories that are handed down from the past that may be based on fact but are not always completely true

**library director** a person in charge of managing a library's staff

**lilacs** plants with sweet-smelling pink, purple, or white flowers

**locks** curls of hair

**lofts** spaces that are inside rooms and are raised up toward the roof or ceiling

**mansion** a very large and grand house

**manuscripts** books that are written by hand

**mausoleum** a large tomb that sits aboveground, where a dead body is housed

**memorial** something that is built to remember a person who has died

**mischief** playful behavior that may cause trouble

**morgue** a place where dead bodies are kept before being buried

**patrons** people who use the services offered by a business

**professors** people who teach at colleges or universities

**psychics** people who can communicate with the spirits of the dead

**seminary** a school at or above the high school level

**sheet music** musical notes printed on sheets of paper

**spirit** a supernatural being, such as a ghost

**stained-glass window** a window made of colored glass

**trestle** a bridge that holds up something, such as railroad tracks

# Read More

**Chandler, Matt.** *Famous Ghost Stories of North America (Haunted World).* North Mankato, MN: Capstone Press, 2019.

**Hollihan, Kerrie Logan.** *Ghosts Unveiled! (Creepy and True).* New York: Abrams Books for Young Readers, 2020.

**Snowden, Matilda.** *Investigating Ghosts in Schools (Investigating Ghosts).* Hallandale, FL: Mitchell Lane Publishers, 2021.

**Wood, Alix.** *Spooky Schools (World's Scariest Places).* New York: Gareth Stevens Publishing, 2020.

# Learn More Online

1. Go to **www.factsurfer.com** or scan the QR code below.

2. Enter "**Eerie Education**" into the search box.

3. Click on the cover of this book to see a list of websites.

# Index

Augusta State University 22-23
Bard College 6-7
Baylor University 10-11
Bennington College 30-31
Billings, Frederick 28
Billings, Parmly 28
Boston University 14
Brand, Leslie Coombs 20-21
Brand Library 20-21
Bridgeport Public
    Library 36-37
Browning, Elizabeth
    Barrett 10-11
Browning, Robert 10-11
Carnegie, Andrew 17
Carnegie Library 16-17
Carpenter, Louise 8-9
Carpenter, Willard 8
Civil War 23
Cramer, Jacob Frank 33
Fordham University 26-27
Fuchs, Joseph 21
Galt, Emily 23
Grey Lady 8-9, 43
Haskell, Harriet 12-13
*Haunting of Hill House,
    The* 30-31
Jackson, Shirley 30-31
Julia Ideson Library 32-33

Kenyon College 34-35
Lewis and Clark Community
    College 13
Lola 37
Millicent Library 24-25
Monticello Seminary 12-13
Morehouse, Bill 39
Muse of Poetry 25
O'Neill, Eugene 14-15
Parmly Billings Library 28-29
Petey 33
Pierson, Stuart 35
Ramona Convent Secondary
    School 40-41
Reid Memorial Library 12
Rogers, Henry Huttleston 25
Rogers, Millicent 25
San Francisco Art
    Institute 38-39
Trans-Allegheny
    Bookstore 16-17
Twain, Mark 25
University of Tampa 18-19
Welden, Paula 31
Willard Library 8-9
Zabriskie, Captain
    Andrew C. 7

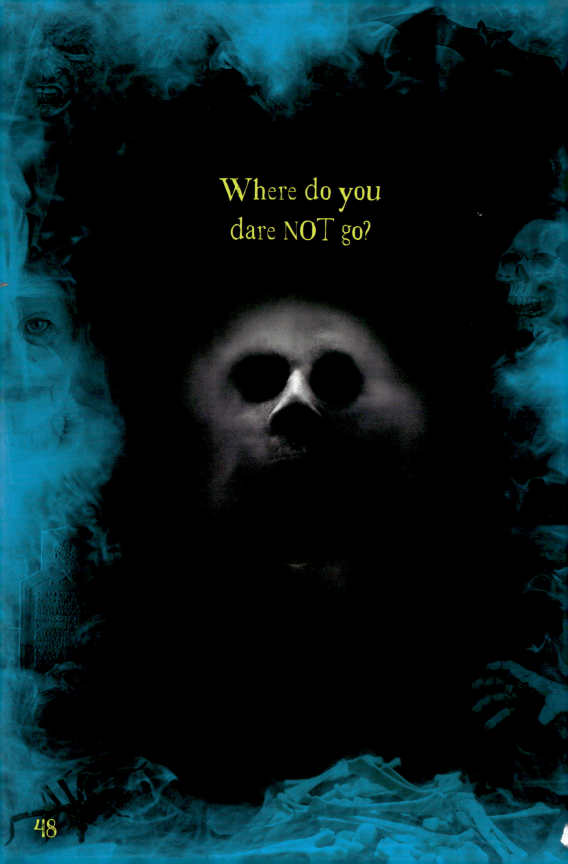